For our daughter, Lailah Alyse Johnson,
I love you always/already.

AIN'T NEVER NOT BEEN BLACK

poems by

Javon Johnson

Published by Button Poetry / Exploding Pinecone Press
Minneapolis, MN 55403 | http://www.buttonpoetry.com

CONTENTS

AIN'T NEVER
NOT BEEN
BLACK

UNTITLED, OR A FEAR OF GIVING THIS A NAME

I start this with a simple confession:

I wanted to burn
this country down.

BLACK 201

Thoughts on Survival
Meeting: All Day, Errrrday

Professor: Javon L. Johnson
Semester: ALL
Office Hours: By Appointment Only
Office Phone: N/A
Office Location: Zora Neale Hurston Hall 241
Email: jjohnson@jamesbaldwin.edu

Course Description: When the white man at the breakfast bar starts rapping "I'm going going back back to Cali Cali" because after small talk you told him you're on your way home to California, you wonder if he does this to other white people. Your Black experiences tell you he likely does not. You pray he stops talking. He does not. You want to check him, but you are certain that being the only Black guy in a room of white people checking the "well-meaning" white guy would likely get you labeled. Angry. Hostile. Anti-white (whatever that means). Crazy. As if racism isn't a thing. You decide today to swallow this foolishness, to let it die somewhere deep inside you. This is also unhealthy. This is all so BLACK. This is also a lesson in survival.

Required Texts:
Alexander, Michelle. *The New Jim Crow*
Baldwin, James. *Notes of a Native Son*
Carter-Knowles, Beyonce. *Lemonade*
Ellison, Ralph. *Invisible Man*
Lorde, Audre. *Sister Outsider: Essays and Speeches*
Public Enemy. *It Takes a Nation of Millions to Hold Us Back*
Simone, Nina. Every song she's ever sung
Touré. *The Portable Promised Land*
  • And a bunch of other really Black shit.

Methods of Evaluations / Course Requirements:
- Be BLACK
- Be real BLACK
- Be all kinds of BLACK

Course Schedule: This course will be mad fluid. This course operates on CPT. This is also a lesson in survival. BLACK.

NEAR DEATH

did I ever tell you about the time I nearly died?
my Mother, my Black mother, my five-foot
skyscraper of a mother, tells the story much better
than I do. she says I stopped breathing for so long
that my face turned blue. she says she didn't know
what to do with me. says she gave me to her mother,
my four-ten cotton hammer of a Grandmother.
she says she has no clue what Grandmother did,
that she must have worked some Black girl magic,
some survival tactic she must've gotten from her mother
who learned it from her mother before her,
and so on. and I think that is an interesting way
to say she could have been a medical doctor
if not for the way the world tries to chew Black
women with its mouth wide open. no manners.
greedy and never full.

WISHING WELL

When my mother tells me to get home
safe, her voice is the last coin she owns
and (nearly) everything is a wishing well.
She is praying to any god she can find
that an officer does not make a hashtag out of me,
does not make me body-bag beautiful.

AMERICA

In this poem,
Black people will be replaced
by the word America.

America has a deep history,
can trace its roots
before colonial expansion, you know.
Refuses to be reduced
to the slave trade.
America never needed a Declaration
of Independence
to know that all "are created equal."
America knows that. Knows that
Lincoln did not free the slaves,
knows, in fact, America did.
America remembers the Civil War,
the Reconstruction Era,
The Birth of a Nation, and
Jim Crow. Knows the KKK.
America loves its hoods
but hates the hood.
America remembers
the Civil Rights Era.
Remembers all the wars.
America is always at war.
But is not as violent
as the world thinks.
America has to protect itself,
has to drop bombs. America is the bomb.
Changed history.
America is the history, the present, and
the future.
Oh, America, the beautiful,
sleight of hand,
quicker than the eye

the way they dodge blades,
ropes, and chains,
how they constantly
pull rabbits out of the hat.
Listen. America.
Penn & Teller caught bullets
in their teeth in front of a live audience—
it is widely accepted
as one of the most brilliant magic tricks
in all of human history.
America is full of magicians,
the way they stay catching bullets.
The greatest illusion,
how the trick is replicated.
We see Black—
I mean, American bodies
disappear
every week,
yet there's never blood on anyone's hands.
Abracadabra! Reappear.
One Black—I mean, American
video down and the next one shows up.
America hates their niggas.
America loves their niggas.
America is niggas.
And when Black people—
I mean, America has had enough,
we will burn this motherfucker down,
sip tea, call it a party, a revolution.
America is a revolution.
America is pimps and prostitutes,
preachers and professionals.
The first time
I knew I was American,
I went camping.
I was surrounded
by two little white girls
and one little white boy

in what had to be
the cutest little Klan rally
you ever wanted to see.
The air was a "whites Only" sign.
They called me nigger like
they knew something I did not.
I marched away
as peaceful as I knew how.
Oh, America,
imagine the weather
that Bloody Sunday.
How the arrogant sun
had the nerve to still rise
the next morning.
America is always in mourning.
One nation under
God. Wizards,
how they constantly pull niggas
out of hats and smile
a confetti of bullets.
The misdirection
makes us lose sight
of all the reasons
they needed niggas
in the first place.

Please remember,
in this poem
America was always
America.

CHOKE

You choke from the blood
on your own hands
then blame those
too arrogant to bleed
properly after you murder them.

America is such a strange liberator.

BLACKBOYS/COLD

it is a 30 degree night/in the middle of the desert/and this is the coldest/weather us boys from South Central/had ever experienced/we were 16/maybe/17/or maybe 18/i don't know/we were men/maybe/Black boys are never allowed to be just/Black boys/and i think about South Central/and that one time we stripped our friend naked/just to laugh at the fact/he hadn't grown pubes yet/and ain't that funny/that he was not yet a man/that he was still growing/that he was too weak/to stop all of us/that we were predators/that we already knew how to do america's work/that he was too stupid to grow pubes/yet/ten years later my cousin tried to fight me/over a card/game/and months before that/an "educated" white man accused me of playing/the race card/because i was savage/in my response to his racism/because i don't play games anymore/because america is too cold/because i know what happens to "weak" boys/and i am a man/maybe/and isn't that what being Black is all about/how the world works to reduce you/even if you only want freedom

AND . . .

my single mother raised
two Black boys in gang ridden,
crack infested 1980s south central,
los angeles. when speaking of us,
she often says, "I'm so happy
my boys are still alive,
not in jail. They're doing well."
she never starts with my phd from northwestern,
my brother's master's in business from usc.
she knows how easy our graduations
could have been funerals.
all pomp and circumstance. being a Black
mother means playing russian roulette
every time you send your kids out
the front door for school, for skittles and tea,
for groceries,
or to just . . .

CUZ HE'S BLACK

"cuz he's black & poor
he's disappeared
the name waz lost"
– Ntozake Shange

I am driving down the street
with my 5-year-old nephew.
He, knocking back a juice
box, me, a Snapple, today
y'all, we are doing some real
manly shit. I love watching
his mind work. He asks
a million questions:
Uncle, how come the sky is blue?
Uncle, how do cars go?
Uncle, why can't dogs talk?
Uncle, uncle, uncle, he asks,
uncle, uncle, uncle, he asks
uncle repeatedly as if his voice box
is a warped record. I try my best
to answer every question.
It's because the way the sun lights up outer space.
It's because the engines make the wheels go.
It's because their brains aren't quite like ours.
Yes. Yes. No. Yes. No. No. I don't know.
Who knows? Maybe.
He smiles at me, then
looks out the window,
spots a cop car,
drops his seat, and says,
"Aww man, Uncle, 5-0, we gotta hide."

I yell at him, "Get up.
In this car, in this family,
we are not afraid

of the law."
I wonder if he hears
the uncertainty in my voice.

We both know the truth
is far more complex than
do not hide. We both know
Black boys disappear. Names lost.
Both know this is no accident.
It's a mass lynching in auto tune
and on auto drive.
Know too many Trayvon Martins,
Oscar Grants, too many Sean Bells,
Abner Louimas, and Amadou Diallos.
Know too well that we are
the hard-boiled sons of Emmett Till.
Still we both know
it's not about whether or not
the shooter is racist—
it's about how poor Black boys
are treated as problems well
before we are treated as people.

Black boys can't afford to play cops
and robbers when we're
always considered the latter,
don't have the luxury of playing war
when we're already in one.

Where I'm from, seeing cop cars
drive down the street feels a lot
like low flying planes in New York
City. Police
sirens become a soundtrack to a horror film,
reminding us that tragedy isn't far away.
Routine traffic stops are more
like mine fields—any wrong moves
could mean your life.

How do I look my nephew in his apple face
and tell him to stand up
for himself when we both know Black boys
are murdered every day simply for being
strong. I tell him be careful. Be smart. Know your laws.
Be courteous, be aware of
how quickly your hands move
to pocket for wallet or ID, be
even more aware of how quickly
the officer's hand moves to holster for gun.
Be Black. Be a boy and have fun
because this world will force you to
become a man much quicker
than you should ever have the need to.

"But Uncle," he asks,
face full of tomorrow.
"Uncle, what happens
if the cop is really mean?"

And it scares me to
know that he, like
so many Black boys,
is getting ready for a war
I can't prepare him for.

ON THE MURDER OF BLACK CHILDREN

I want to live in a world
where the police do not murder Black children.

Where the police do not murder Black children.
Where the police do not murder Black children.
Where the police do not murder Black children.
Where the police do not murder Black children.
Where the police do not murder Black children.
Where the police do not murder Black children.
Where the police do not murder Black children.
Where the police do not murder Black children.
Where the police do not murder Black children.
Where the police do not murder Black children.
Where the police do not murder Black children.
Where the police do not murder Black children.
Where the police do not murder Black children.
Where the police do not murder Black children.
Where the police do not murder Black children.
Where the police do not murder Black children.
Where the police do not murder Black children.
Where the police do not murder Black children.
Where the police do not murder Black children.
Where the police do not murder Black children.

Where the police do not murder Black children.
Where the police do not murder Black children.
Where the police do not murder Black children.
Where the police do not murder Black children.
Where the police do not murder Black children.

Where the police do not murder Black children.
Where *the* police do not murder Black children.
Where the *police* do not murder Black children.
Where the police *do* not murder Black children.
Where the police do *not* murder Black children.

Where the police do not *murder* Black children.
Where the police do not murder *Black* children.
Where the police do not murder Black *children.*

Where the police do not murder Black children.
Where the police do not murder Black children.
Where the police do not murder Black children.
Where the police do not murder Black children.
Where the police do not murder Black children.
Where the police do not murder Black children.

Where the police do not murder BLACK CHILDREN.
Where the police do not murder BLACK CHILDREN.
Where the police do not murder BLACK CHILDREN.
Where the police do not murder BLACK CHILDREN.
Where the police do not murder BLACK CHILDREN.

I want to live in a world
where the police do not murder Blackchildren.
where the police do not murder Blackchildren.
where the police do not murder Blackchildren.
where the police do not murder Blackchildren.
where the police do not murder Blackchildren.
where the police do not murder Blackchildren.
where the police do not murder Blackchildren.
where the police do not murder Blackchildren.
where the police do not murder Blackchildren.

I want to live in a world where the police do not murder Black
    children.
I want to live in a world where the police do not murder Black . . .
I want to live in a world where the police do not murder . . .
I want to live in a world where the police do not . . .

I want to live.
I want to.

EVERYONE HAD NICKNAMES WHERE I GREW UP

Banos, Big Brown, Cheese, Crook,
E. Love, Pep, Spooky Blood.

███████ was a killer and a hood pharmacist.
We grew up in church together, he and I.
His grandmother was strict.
He was such a good boy on Sundays.

What is it for Black boys to live two lives
when the world does not want us to live

one?

BLACK *AND* HAPPY

On the night they decided not to indict
Darren Wilson for the cold-
blooded murder of Mike Brown
I, a well-framed riot,
chose not to protest. Instead
I shut down
everything and like
any good gospel conductor
demanded a better harmony.

The protests were in a part of Oakland
I walk to almost every day, but on that night,
I closed the windows, could not deal
with yet another choir lifting the rafters
about more Black death.
I didn't want to be sad,
didn't want white supremacy
to tell me how to feel again. Instead
I fell asleep smiling, listening
to Nina Simone and Otis Redding.
That night, I cut off all the lights
cause Black was the only god
worth praying to. Asked if
Jesus was a Black woman,
said, the only people I know
who could stretch that small amount of food
into a feast are big mommas. We laughed.
Talked about bones and spades, about
how Black women must be magic.
Couldn't figure out why
all the old Black men who smoke menthols
know how to fix carburetors, too. Smiled at
how creative Black kids are.
This world ain't never been safe
so we build new ones

out of bones, scrap paper, and possibility.
Funny how we make survival look stylish,
look dope, look damned good. We dance on beat.
That night I chose to be happy AND Black.

When I first saw a man shot
to death, his arms flailed wildly
as if he danced for a God he knew
he would see. What an unholy prayer
his body was, arms were in the wrong
direction. But this poem isn't
about Black death; it's
about how that night we listened
to Tupac, imagined heaven's ghetto.
Corner stores draped in gold. An ocean
of Black faces smiled as wide as before
the beginning, when it was still Black
and was still good. Little girls played Double
Dutch, and him, still dancing.

When I awoke the next morning
to an arrogant sun, I called my mother
because Black is the only gospel song
still worth singing. We laughed
and said, "I love you."
I wanted her to know
her baby boy was both Black and alive.

But this cannot be
about politics, cannot be
about Black on Black
crime, or the prison industrial complex.
This is not a metaphor;
it is simply about Black love.
About cookouts and fish frys
where all the Black kids
know the dances before
they entered the world. About

how Black folks wear gold
crowns in our mouths
cause we have regular brushes with royalty.
This is about how at times
the most revolutionary thing I can do
is enjoy my nieces' laughter.
Their brown faces and the way
their smiles bubble
like good fried bologna sandwiches.
And ain't that Black, y'all?

This is about how
when my brother came home
from his tour in Iraq
the first thing we did was hug and
make fun of each other.
When Tamir Rice was gunned down,
Black people banded together
to help his mother out
of the homeless shelter she was in.
When my aunt lay in her deathbed,
waiting for cancer
to finally make her lungs a liar
out of her own body,
she still cracked jokes.
You cannot kill Blackness;
too much of it is wrapped in unshakable joy.
And ain't that why they think we magic
in the first place?
That despite every reason not to,
we still love.
We still Black, y'all.
We still.

BLACK FAMOUS (A FAUX HAIKU SERIES)

I just want to be
Black famous. With a show on
BET, you know.

AN OPEN LETTER TO TIGER WOODS

Dear Tiger,

You never knew
nigger sounds
the way it does,
did you? Strategically
forgot Fuzzy Zoeller's "fried chicken"
comments when they
draped that green
jacket on your back and
called you Master. They
pulled a fast one on
you, slipped you a mickey. And
now they got you
dancing, boy,
like you the only nigga
that knows
the swing. Had us all
watching the right
hand while your left
played tricks with melodies, or
whatever
their names were.
John Shippen, 1896, was
the first Black
person to play in the US
Open. He had to register
as a Shinnecock Indian.
In 1962, Charlie Sifford
became the first Black
PGA Tour member. Lee Elder
in 1975 was the first African
-American to play at
the Masters in Augusta. It wasn't

until 1990 that Augusta National would
admit its first Black member.

Tiger, the coon-
hounds are
a-coming, and there
are no coffins
for your wounds. No place
to hide. You
stand there and
take it—"good"
colored boys are broken
that way. This
is what
a high-tech lynching
feels like. What
a nigga down
an Alabama back
road, minus the Alabama
or the back road, feels
like. What Emmett
Till's mother already knew. Colored
boys ain't got no reason
to be smiling
'round pretty white
women less they be holding
their bags or
opening car doors and even
then we know well
to do a careful but awkward
two-step. The white-gloved "good Negro"
dance. This is Jim Crow
in HD; a "whites only" sign
digitally remastered and hung
in Dolby. Strong white
boys cut their teeth on shit
like this—ask

your father. Major
sports have always had issues
with colored boys,
spooks,
coons who break color
barriers in Kansas or Mississippi.

You got to feel what it's like
to be OJ. You would have thought
you'd slit that white woman's throat
the way they blackface
minstreled you
across our television screens.
Ask Frederick Douglass—
breaking proud
niggas has always been good
for this economy. They chew colored boys.
Cannibals, they are.
They made an example out of you.

BLACK FAMOUS 2

Perhaps I could be
number 2 or 3 on the
barbershop posters.

THE LAST CONVERSATION BETWEEN MALCOLM X AND HIS DAUGHTER

Baby girl,
today I am sure
men with serrated faces
and callused smiles
will come for me.
These men with their
half-chewed hearts
have been watching me.
They tap our phones.
Read our mail.
Illegally look at our finances.
Hell, they even called your mother,
personally,
to tell her they are to kill me. And
they will kill me.

You are to act like I
have always taught you to.
You are to smile and laugh,
to be strong and have pride.
You are to know
your history. Remember
me as I am because
these men who speak
in creative truths will say
I defied Elijah Muhammad
but will say nothing about the children
he fathered with teenaged girls.
They will say I wanted to be bigger
than the Black Muslim movement but
will say nothing about how
I wanted Black freedom to be the religion.
They will try
to convince you I am monster.

Like I've never held you
or told you bedtime
stories. Like I never checked in
your closet for monsters,
or underneath beds.
Like I've never
looked you in the face
and promised you sky.
Like I've never sat there
with clumsy hands,
braided your hair
and kissed you beautiful.
Like I've never
kissed your mother's lips
or said I love you.
Like I was never
a husband, or
a father, or
a brother, or
a son. Like I don't have
a mother. Like I don't
smile. Like I don't know God.

Baby girl,
these men with shrapnel
for hands will try to
convince you I am crazy,
as if freedom isn't something
worth fighting for.
They will tell
you they did this
because no one man should
have all of this power.

They won't tell you
they did this
because I am Malcolm Little.
Turned Detroit Red.

Turned Malcolm X.
Turned El-Hajj Malik El-Shabazz.
Because I am bad.
I am a bad muthafucka.

These men
are the same types of men
who brought you the deaths
of Patrice Lumumba,
of Medgar Evers, and JFK
in laser quality, and they
will try to convince you
I am a mad man,
like I never held or kissed you.
Like I'm not a father.
Like. I'm. Not. Your. Father.

Baby girl,
remember that morning
about two weeks ago?
You looked at me,
your eyes were so brown,
you asked,
"Daddy, how come
you didn't drink all
of your coffee today?"
I didn't want to
tell you it got cold.
So instead I took your finger,
swirled it in my cup,
drank every last drop,
and then told you,
"It needed a little more brown
sugar." Remember how big you smiled?

Today these men
will try to take your smile.
They will say they assassinated

Malcolm X, a Muslim extremist,
a civil rights leader. You
will say they murdered
your father, who
will never see you graduate
or get married if you so choose,
who will not be there
when they ask, "Who
gives this woman away?" I
don't want to give you away.
I'm sorry
I will never hold your
children, will never know
their names.

But today these men with their rope
and shotgun justice will come
hunting for a monster.
Baby girl, show the world
how they killed a human being.

BLACK FAMOUS 3

One day I'll show up
to see *Cats* on Broadway and
yell, "What's good, nigga?"

THE SAMO

For Jean-Michel Basquiat

It should come as
no surprise then
that an economy built
on chattel slavery
and the selling
and purchasing of Black bodies,
that white people would go wild
in buying your primitive
nigga art. You
greatest of freak
shows. You whispering
nuclear warhead. You wild
haired Negro who painted
Armani suits beautiful
again. Walked red
carpets and gallery
openings with a crumbling Haiti
splattered across your
face, the Kompa
barely able to hold up
your eyes. Puerto Rico stuffed
in the back of your throat,
protected behind the Africa
in your smile. Brooklyn
never knew what they had, never
knew the Bomba dancing in
your fingertips, never knew
once you walked across that water
you'd become god. You
poet of a painter
you. Storyteller with a song
worth bleeding for. They
bought your work by the
dozens in the same places

they bought niggas
who were whipped,
crack-backed by
the dozens. Yo momma
ain't laughing no
more. Funny how you were
a banker's son but never fully realized
your worth. You always knew
you were on an auction block.
The greatest
trick slave owners
ever pulled was convincing us all
that niggas were no longer
for sale. Like team
owners don't sit in
skyboxes looking
down on their fields, ready
to trade their big money making niggas whenever
they speak out or
when their bodies begin to fail or
when they ask for their worth.
As if the field
mobs in Cleveland
didn't burn, hang
even, LeBron James jerseys
because they couldn't
bring home their most prized runaway.

Jean-Michel,
did they tell you
they'd never stop
selling you? That
your Blackness is forever
on a chopping block?
Like Malcolm X
caps or Africa
engraved leather
medallions. Like Martin's

dream. Like Garvey
and the Black Panther
Party. No wonder
you lost yourself.
You were chasing that
dragon when
all you needed was us
to show you
your way home.
I'm sorry
we waited far
too late to hold you
to the heavens,
forgot how to tell you that
you are royalty,
when all you did
was have the courage
to celebrate Black
Kings when
the world forgot how.

BLACK FAMOUS 4

Not too famous though.
Don't want to be a hashtag.
No twitter coffins.

THE CULT OF OBAMA

On the morning
of the 2008 presidential election,
my grandfather,
whose whisper is
as quiet as a musty bar fight,
whose grandparents were
slaves, called me and said,
"Boy, I'm sure is just happy
to see a Black man
got a real shot. You know?"
I responded, "No G-pops,
he has to win."
The following morning
I went to Memphis
for a show. I decided
to go the National Civil Rights Museum.
Built at the Lorraine Motel,
the last stop is the balcony
where Dr. Martin Luther King Jr. was assassinated.

To understand the Cult of Obama,
why so many (Black)
people are unwilling to critique
the president
even amidst the drone strikes,
the mass surveillance, the deportations,
his continued need to call out Black "dysfunction,"
and the Home Affordable Modification Program that helped
big banks more than Black families,
you have to go to Memphis
and see that Dr. King's blood is still on the ground.

BLACK FAMOUS 5

Not too famous though.
I just want people to think,
He's familiar.

LOS ANGELES

Los Angeles is a gospel song my grandmother used to sing.
A dream my grandfather left Louisiana for.
A roach coach turned fusion food truck.
And this, too, is cosmetic surgery.
The imported palm trees.
The way they open themselves up for an always smiling sun.

Los Angeles is a car on the front lawn.
A jagged gold toothed truth.
And didn't we all rush here for a piece of the pie?

Los Angeles is a confusing parking sign.
It does not know if it wants you to stay here or go.
And ain't that part of its magic?
It is home to my mother's cooking.
Where we learned to cook coke to crack.
We build up our stars to bury them in the ground.
And, still, it is a city that is not wrapped up in Hollywood.

N.W.A

Back in the 80s,
when niggas poisoned the streets just as they did their hair,
Niggaz With Attitude came
"Straight Outta Compton" with sawed-offs, gats, AK47s, and
     automatics.

They, too, put chemicals in their hair
to make it relax or curl.
And indeed there is a lazy metaphor there
about the colonization of our minds, but
that says nothing about how they left their Kings
hats sweaty and greasy—I'm guessing
niggas preferred their starter crowns dirty.

My ███████, a real-life gangster,
a gun-toting-drug dealing-street-running-chipped-tooth
-scarred-knuckled-gangster,
introduced me to them.
He played "Fuck tha Police."
He, knowing my mother is a saved woman,
a church-going-big-hat-wearing-tambourine-playing
-scripture-quoting woman,
said, "Don't get lost in the cursing—get lost in the message."

And I immediately knew that
they didn't hate these niggas because they were vile or violent;
they hated them because they were niggas
or niggas with audacity
or niggas with authority
or niggas we admired for simply being niggas
or niggas that did not give a fuck.

And ain't that a kind of liberation?
Ain't that somewhat close to freedom?

ON LEARNING FREEDOM

The first time I slow danced with a girl was at a backyard party in South Central. It was a sweaty night and the air was too thick for anything but a slow song. I wore my flyest silk shirt, a thin gold chain that danced around my neck as if it understood music more than I did. I had a cup full of Hawaiian Punch and 7Up in my right hand. My back was against the wall. I was watching all those Black kids learning to get free. Quiet as kept, I was always afraid of dancing, of girls. Just then SWV's "Weak" came on and Tasha yelled, "This is my song!" as if she wrote it. And to this day, I still want to believe her. Tasha, a dark-skinned Black girl who wore thick scrunchy socks, air brushed t-shirts, hoops, who kept her ponytail on the right side of her head. A few weeks earlier, Oatmeal told me Tasha liked me, and I came to the party to show her how I cool I was. Our friends forced us together, and as she swayed her hips, Oatmeal grabbed me and made me move mine. He whispered in my ear, "You got this." Once everyone stopped watching me fumble my way through the song, Tasha told me to keep my hands around her hips. She held me and carefully taught me how to feel the beat, how to feel the rhythm, you know, how to move.

199SOMETHING

That was the summer they decided to cut
the public pool hours at Ross Snyder's Park.

That was also the summer we saw the death toll rise,
when we lost so many smiling Black kids.

I guess when you can't beat the heat, you pull it.

A LESSON IN PROPER SENTENCE CONSTRUCTION

Writing is a process
where you place sentences
in a sequence.
Whenever a single
sentence is read aloud,
it should be comprehensible.
Example: I have a really big smile. See.
A sentence is a group of words
used to impart meaning and
is constructed according to the rules of grammar.
Coherent and concise sentences
are almost always preferable.
Example: Javon smiles. See.
Javon is the proper noun
but can be easily replaced
in the following sentences
by the noun *boy*.
Smiles is the action verb;
it does something in the world.
You can also throw in an adjective—
they're usually placed just before the noun.
Example: The Black boy smiles.
Adverbs, on the other hand,
should always follow the verb they describe.
Example: The Black boy smiles largely. See.

However, it should be noted
that the Black boy in this sentence
is the sentence
but not the sentenced.
The Black boy is
not a lesson about court cases or
how the judicial system railroads
Black families. In this poem,
the Black boy is the subject;

the sentence is the object.
The object lesson being that
the court constructs its sentences
opposite grammatical law.
It is incorrect for a judge to say,
"I'm going to go with the State's
recommendation and sentence you
to X amount of years."
Rather, a judge should use present
perfect tense for the unfinished past.
Which is to say,
when we discuss things
that have already happened and
consider the time
in which they occurred to be unfinished,
we use present tense conjugation.
Therefore, a judge might say,
"The state has been recommending and
sentencing the Black boy for years."

I once thought I wanted to conquer
the world, which is to say,
like any mediocre white man
we later call great, I thought
my life worthy of a state
sanctioned monument,
which is to say, I was a model citizen.
Pledged allegiance. Believed
the American Dream and U.S. justice.
Years ago, I testified in court as
a character witness for a friend.
Thought my degrees would matter.
The judge gave him almost 10 years
for a felony he likely did not commit.
But even if he did,
What exactly does that sentence say?
What does that sentence mean?
What does it do?

His mother wept uncontrollably,
her face a broken levee
that no president ever cared about.
The courtroom
was a parade of whiteness.
Before they took him away,
he turned to us, but
the Black boy could not smile.
The Black boy could not smile.
The Black boy could not smile.
And isn't that a proper sentence, too?
Clear and concise. But somehow still
longer like the sentences
Black people are given.
However, the Black boy was jailed
is incorrect; it is passive and lacks a subject.
Who jailed the Black boy?
Who jailed the Black boy?
Who is responsible for jailing the Black boy?
The racist system jailed him harshly.
See how easily
he was moved from subject to object.
See the placement of the adjective, noun, verb, and adverb.
See who's doing the action.
See no mention of the Black girl,
how easily she was erased.
See exactly how
to construct a proper sentence.

EVERYTHING I KNOW ABOUT GENTRIFICATION
I LEARNED FROM MY STEP/FATHER, OR WHEN
THE CANCER COMES

When the cancer comes
the experts will gather.
They will say things like,
"I'm afraid there is bad news.
This is not a death sentence.
People live long and normal lives.
We are doing everything we can, but
there is not an exact science to this."
You will only hear, "Bad news.
This is a death sentence."
And you will think,
"We are everything
but not this."

I know cancer is when abnormal cells grow
and spread very quickly. These cells
group together, forming tumors,
destroying the normal cells, and
causing damage to the body's healthy tissues.
Sometimes cancer cells break away
from the tumor, destroying
other parts of the body, and
this is the best definition of gentrification
that I have.

I live in Oakland
where those in charge of the city are
building up new sky-rises
quicker than they can
tear down old Black bodies.
Death by crooked cop or
crooked crane is all the same.

Gentrification is killing us.
The abnormal cells are spreading
too quickly. They are
grouping together. Forming tumors.
Destroying the body.
When the new Oakland residents call
the cops on the drum circle
filled with people of color,
they are trying to stop the Black heartbeat.
When they call the cops on the Black church,
which has been here for 65 years,
for being too loud, they are
trying strip Oakland of its soul.
To gentrify is to take the body
and gut it. It is
to treat the entire city like
a chophouse. And these butchers
have no manners.
They do not pray over the slaughtered.
They do not even have the decency
to make use of the entire carcass.
They simply toss out the bones,
as if there is no need to season the stock.
There is no God in this.

My step/father is a pastor, and
before that he was a deacon, and
before that a football coach, and
before that he was a truck driver
who delivered food items.
He is a log cabin of a father,
a patient, high-yellow man
who sings like
he's calling the cattle home.
He thinks his voice is better
than what it is.
Eventually it will go

the way of the house
he raised us in: all memory but
no longer ours; no longer here.

When my mother told me
of his lymphoma,
that he only has a few months to live,
I immediately thought of the newly constructed
mixed-income high-rise built
just up the street. The city does not care
that lower income families cannot afford
a 10-dollar cup of coffee or to shop
at the Whole Foods. The cancer does not care
that the body will never be whole again or
that the body has a family.
The city does not care about Black families or
that Black bodies will be made to feel foreign,
and strange, and out of place;
that the only city they have ever called home
will become too expensive to even breathe in.
At this rate, we will have to lower our dead
into grounds they could not afford
to live on. At some point,
mixed-income housing only prolongs
the inevitable, and this is
the best definition of chemotherapy I have.

Meanwhile, my step/father passed,
and no one asked
the important questions.
How did we get here?
Why is the body eating itself alive?
And where did the God go?

I am a broken prayer
in a burned down church house;
without him I never would have made it,
which is to say, I am Black and I feel

helpless. And this is exactly what cancer does;
it pushes the God out of the body, and
sometimes that body has neighborhoods
for limbs, which is to say,
I will soon watch my step/father die.

When I played football for him and
we lost the semi-final game,
he said to me, "You can't get that one back.
Yeah. I know it hurts.
Cry it out if you have to, but
keep your head up.
Figure out a way to get them next time."
He is everything I know
about gentrification, everything
I can tell you about what happens
when cancer comes.

WHEN THE STATE DECIDES TO MURDER

WHEN the State decides to murder
its next Black child,
do not protest in silence,
do not sing
"We Shall Overcome." Remind them
of the shotgun
in your throat, tell them
THERE WILL BE NO MORE.

Do not tell their mother that
everything will be ok.
It will NOT.
Her chest will be an empty rum barrel,
a broken whiskey bottle,
an oversung gospel song.
She will manage to go on, Black
folks seem to always do,
but who should have to go on like this?

The father will [redacted]
be strong. He will fight back
tears in public. He will cry
in a backroom or
in his basement or
somewhere else safe
like that. He will probably listen
to Marvin, or Miles, or Etta,
or Roberta and Donny, or
someone else safe
like that.

Reimagine the vigils.
Think about the irony in cutting
down yet another flower
to honor that child's beautiful life.

Pay close attention
WHEN the State says,
"This is a time for peace."
They are admitting
that when they first
fired the gun
it was a time of war.
Do not sit quiet.
Do not whisper, unless it's for strategy.
Do not make another Black ballad
to be used in the soundtrack
to another shitty movie about racism
three decades from now. Do not go gentle.
Do not turn the other cheek.
Yell. Scream. Show them
your claws. Your fangs.
Be the monster
they always thought you were.
Show them the anger.
The hurt.
The hurt.
It hurts.
IT hurts.
IT IIURTS.
IT HURTS.
IT HURTS.

ON HEALTHY MASCULINITY

I'm told it took me longer than normal
to unclench my fist
as a newborn. My mother says
this was how she knew
I would be a fighter.

When I was seven, I broke a kid's arm
in two places after he had just beat me up
because my older brother
ordered me to fight him again.

By the time I was 10,
I was championed
for knocking other kids
unconscious on the football field.

When I was 13,
I averaged about three fights a month.
One because a boy looked at me too long,
another because a boy was bold
enough to call my mother a bitch,
a few because I was bored, and
many I can't remember why.
In high school, I was shot at a few times,
fought some more, chocked a boy,
slapped a few others, and kicked one
down the stairs because he disrespected my cousin.

I don't think you understand though.
I am not proud of this.
I want desperately to perform
a healthier masculinity, but
this world has never allowed me
to unclench my fists.

I was 21 in Mississippi
when a truck full of white boys drunk
on Confederate flags,
their eyes, burning crosses;
tongues, nooses;
stopped and called me nigger and boy.
I remember wanting to show them
how much of a nigga I can be,
so I put my back up against the only wall I could find,
put my fists up, and said, "Do what you gotta do."
These hands are rated E for everybody, and
I heard just how much white boys love to play catch.
Just then a cop pulled up and
asked them if I was causing trouble.
They said nothing, but their silence said everything.
Later I told my white college buddy,
and he said, "Good Lord, Javon,
do you know you could've been seriously injured?"
And I thought, ain't that just like a white boy
to remind me that I could always be hurt?
And I wonder,
how different is my buddy from the cop,
both of them from the boys?
And the boys are always around.
So my uncle taught me to walk circumspectly,
to keep my fists clenched,
to make the most of an opportunity, and
swing these hands like good scripture.
Once he told me, and I quote,
"If someone tests you, pray and
remind that nigga of the rapture."
So I swear, I'm only trying to do God's work.

But when my niece tells me
I am the best uncle in the world,
which I am certain she says
to all of her uncles, I know

it is not fists but
the way they bloom into flowers
that makes her say that.

To garden is to dig your hands in the soil,
it is to get dirt underneath your fingernails
and pray that something beautiful springs up.
They say dandelions, though commonly disregarded
as a weed, are completely edible sources of vitamins,
and one cup can produce 7 to 13,000 units of vitamin A.
And this teaches me that even
unwanted things can be useful, too.
Someday I want to be this giving of myself;
I want this unwanted Black boy to feel safe enough
to break open for someone else's health,
but I know that roses have thorns
because some people pick flowers
simply because they can. And
this is the difference between white and
Black masculinities; some days I am the flower,
and others I am shear,
but every day I am vulnerable.
I can be cracked open from the stem or
labeled weapon that must be banned.

I was 35
when a white colleague told me
my anger frightens her.

I was 35
when that same white colleague
praised a while male colleague
for his "passion."

I was 35
when a white family crowded me
after the son proudly said
they can have me arrested.

I was 35
when a cop pulled up and
asked them if I was causing trouble.

I was 35
in a majority white neighborhood
in Oakland when
a white woman asked me
why do I have to be so loud,
to which I replied,
"Why do you have to be in Oakland?"
I was 35
when a guy yelled to her from his balcony
that he's going to call the cops on me.

I was 35
ready to break a motherfucker open.

I was 35, y'all.
I was 35 when my niece grabbed my face
with both of her tiny hands and said,
"Uncle, you're so silly. You're so silly."

And I think, I want to always be the flower.
Fully bloomed. No thorns.

ME

The best way to understand me is
to have my mother's cooking,
too much spice for most people
to stomach, but I like it that way.

On June 8th of 2015, Baron Davis, aka B-Diddy, appeared on ESPN's *First Take* with an S-Curl, and while the entire world made fun of him, I thought to myself, "Good for you, Mr. Davis. Good for you."

AN ODE TO THE S-CURL

Oh, sweet S-Curl.
In the fourth grade
when Aileen said,
"I like boys with that good hair,"
your box became a dirty prayer,
the last confessional I felt comfortable in.
You gave me one Hail Mary
to leave with, hair full of grace, and
ain't that worthy of its own parable?

When Shanteal ran
her hands through my hair
in the eighth grade, you were there.
A pillar in the Black community,
as important to me as hope or a dream.
Always too wet, yet somehow never wet enough.
And ain't that worthy of a parade?

I had my sides faded,
the top curled and hanging over
the edge as niggas
are wont to do.
Back then I kept my sodas in a brown bag
when I drank them because
that's what the men did
with their drinks. They,
the kind of men who called everyone
they did not grow up with "young blood,"
gave me advice about women,
the streets, and
school. Now most of them are gone,
my bald head is a graveyard of follicles, and
I'm not sure what to make of the two.

There might come a day
the kids will know B-Diddy more for his hair
than for his dunks, his crossover, or his acrobatic finishes.
Indeed there might even come a day
the kids will never know the glisten of an S-Curl.
Baron's, an acrobatic finish,
a testament to carefree Black boy joy,
worthy of so much more than a meme.
Mine, a legendary show
worthy of its own Hollywood star.

ENOUGH FOR EVERYBODY, OR MY GRANDMOTHER WAS MY FIRST PHILOSOPHY TEACHER

When we were younger, my grandmother would send us to the corner store to get groceries, candy, and even her cigarettes. When she decided I was old enough to go on my own, she told me, "Go the Fruit Stand and get some collards, a pack Newport 100s, and a thing of lard to cook lunch with." When I asked how much greens should I get, she looked at me as only Black grandmothers know how, and said, "Enough for everybody."

ACKNOWLEDGMENTS

Sitting down to write and revise day after day can and does often feel like an isolated and isolating process; however, writing has always been a collective engagement for me. The acknowledgment pages, although "ritualistic," found in so many books are beaming testaments to the notion that writing can be and often is quite communal. From the feedback I received from my friends and colleagues to reading others' work to the editorial process, many eyes and hearts have poured over *Ain't Never Not Been Black*, and I could not be any more thankful.

I must start by thanking the good folks at Button Poetry for creating and providing the platform to house this project. I am so elated to be amongst the wonderful artists already published by Button. Sam Van Cook, thank you for the multiple conversations that initially led to this union. Hanif Abdurraqib has always been a writer whom I deeply cherish, and I am fortunate to have had him as an editor for *Ain't Never Not Been Black*. Hitomi Wong has been nothing short of wonderful in handling production operations. Finally, I want to acknowledge Nikki Clark, the artist who worked on the cover, as well as the rest of the staff whom I may not have had direct contact but in some way worked on this project. Thank you all for your work and energy.

Being an academic who traffics in non-artistic fields frequently means I am not awarded for creative work. My colleagues at UNLV, particularly those in the Interdisciplinary Department of Gender and Ethnic Studies, have been incredibly gracious in the ways they allow me the space to be a creative academic, one who refuses to concede creativity for the critical. I am especially indebted to Mark Padoognpatt (who moved from colleague to close friend) and the department chair Anne Stevens. Thank you all for your support.

I started to take writing more seriously when I discovered Da Poetry Lounge (DPL) in Hollywood, California. I owe so much to the community that Shihan Van Clief, Poetri Smith, Dante Basco, and Gimel Hooper built. I call DPL my home, and in many ways so many people there have become family. I am particularly thankful to Shihan, Donny Jackson, and Yesika Salgado for providing early feedback and for always having my back. I want to thank the Squad: Rudy Francisco, Terisa Siagatonu, and Imani Cezanne. I talk to at least one of you every day, which means you all are now deeply embedded in my life as individuals and as a collective. I cannot imagine my life without all of you, as your work, friendship, and love feeds me. Thank you all for holding me. I love you.

In my first book, I used a good amount of space thanking my mother, mainly because she worked so hard to give me a world that she could not imagine for herself. I want to thank her, as I always do, for forcing the world to open up for me in ways it refused to do so for her, for instilling in me a sense of wonder and wander, and for giving me the desire to open up the world for those who have come and will come after me. In this way, this book is for my nieces and nephews: LaVaughn Johnson, Ashara Mijares, Semaj Sims, Tony Johnson, III, Domi'on Sims, Dominique Sims, Kinganthony Johnson, Darr Muhammad, Izz Muhammad, Hira Muhammad, Venice Johnson, and Milan Johnson. May you all understand this world in ways that I cannot imagine.

To my loving wife Mandy Mejia-Johnson. When we first met, you looked like everything I have ever said yes to. I am a ball of contradictions and you allow me (almost) all of them. You are the first person I have dated to whom I never had to explain my messy. Indeed I want to explain myself to you but that I don't have to makes you feel like home. In many ways, I am the opposite of who I project publicly. I am a frightened and shy boy who desperately wants love, safety, and acceptance. Thank you for providing those things for me, for loving me enough, and for creating the space for me to be a weird loner in one moment and a "normal" person the next. I hope my love is as transformative for you as yours is for me.

ABOUT THE AUTHOR

Javon Johnson is a three-time National Poetry Slam champion, a five-time national finalist, and has appeared on HBO's *Def Poetry Jam*, BET's *Lyric Café*, TV One's *Verses and Flow*, *The Steve Harvey Show*, *The Arsenio Hall Show*, and *United Shades of America with Kamau Bell* on CNN. He also co-wrote a documentary titled *Crossover*, which aired on Showtime, in collaboration with the NBA and Nike. The author of *Killing Poetry: Blackness and the Making of Slam and Spoken Word Communities* (Rutgers University Press, 2017) and the co-editor of *The End of Chiraq: A Literary Mixtape* (Northwestern University Press, 2018), Johnson is an Assistant Professor and the Director of African American & African Diaspora Studies and holds an appointment in Gender & Sexuality Studies in the Interdisciplinary, Gender, and Ethnic Studies Department at the University of Nevada, Las Vegas.

OTHER BOOKS BY BUTTON POETRY

If you enjoyed this book, please consider checking out some of our others, below. Readers like you allow us to keep broadcasting and publishing. Thank you!

Neil Hilborn, *Our Numbered Days*
Hanif Abdurraqib, *The Crown Ain't Worth Much*
Sabrina Benaim, *Depression & Other Magic Tricks*
Rudy Francisco, *Helium*
Rachel Wiley, *Nothing Is Okay*
Neil Hilborn, *The Future*
Phil Kaye, *Date & Time*
Andrea Gibson, *Lord of the Butterflies*
Blythe Baird, *If My Body Could Speak*
Desireé Dallagiacomo, *SINK*
Dave Harris, *Patricide*
Michael Lee, *The Only Worlds We Know*
Raych Jackson, *Even the Saints Audition*
Brenna Twohy, *Swallowtail*
Porsha Olayiwola, *i shimmer sometimes, too*
Jared Singer, *Forgive Yourself These Tiny Acts of Self-Destruction*
Adam Falkner, *The Willies*
Kerrin McCadden, *Keep This To Yourself*
George Abraham, *Birthright*
Omar Holmon, *We Were All Someone Else Yesterday*
Rachel Wiley, *Fat Girl Finishing School*
Nava EtShalom, *Fortunately*
Bianca Phipps, *crown noble*
Rudy Francisco, *I'll Fly Away*

Available at buttonpoetry.com/shop and more!